All Scripture references taken from the KJV of the Holy Bible, unless otherwise indicated.

Gates of Thanksgiving

by Dr. Marlene Miles

Freshwater Press 2023

ISBN: 978-1-963164-00-8

Paperback Version

Copyright 2023, Dr. Marlene Miles

All rights reserved. No part of this book may be reproduced, distributed or transmitted by any means or in any means including photocopying, recording or other electronic or mechanical methods without prior written permission of the publisher except in the case of brief publications or critical reviews.

Table of Contents

Where Have All the Manners Gone? 5

The Arc of Thank You 11

Strongmen or Strongholds at the Gate 14

A Heart of Thanksgiving 21

Let Me In 24

We Are Invited 28

Ungrateful Heart 34

It's A Realm 39

10,000 Tongues 44

Wholeness 49

The Prophetic Thank You 58

Pride Stops It 63

Welcome 66

They Became DEAD 67

He Gave Thanks 70

He Showed Us How 75

The Grace of Thanksgiving 77

The Power of Thanksgiving 81

By His Grace 82

All Day 85

At the Communion Table 86

Except Judas	89
He Took the Bread	91
Dear Reader	95
Other books by this author	96

Gates of Thanksgiving

Where Have All the Manners Gone?

People don't have manners like they used to. People don't say, *thank you* very often anymore even if you do something nice for them.

Most in the world know that grateful people are happier, more content; they experience life in a fuller way, and they have better memories. But, I am presupposing that those with no manners who don't say, *thank you*--, either easily, or at all are not of the household of Christian faith.

Christians are thankful people, well, at least they should be. We should easily show appreciation to others, and especially to God. We should definitely honor those who serve us, because we are also, like Jesus called to be servants.

Thanksgiving is a cornerstone to our faith as we enter into His gates with Thanksgiving and bless His Name.

> Enter into his gates with thanksgiving, and into his courts with praise: be thankful unto him, and bless his name.
>
> For the LORD is good; his mercy is everlasting; and his truth endureth to all generations, (Psalms 100:4-5).

Sometimes when folks can't say, *Thank you,* there are deeper reasons than ingratitude. Jealousy is one such reason. When Joseph's brothers were jealous of him, they could not speak peaceably to him,

And when his brethren saw that their father loved him more than all his brethren, they hated him, and could not speak peaceably unto him. (Genesis 37:4).

Pride, as we will mention later, strongly opposes manners. The prideful do not readily, if ever use words such as, *please*, and *thank you*. On the front end, they think they deserve what they are getting from you and on the back end they can be so narcissistic that they think they did *you* a favor by letting you **serve** them or give them something. Yeah, it's that bad. I was making nachos for a fellow one time, and he said that I should hurry up if I ever wanted to get to cook for him again.

Wait, wait, wait! I like to cook but I don't consider it an honor to cook for someone who is rude, demanding, unappreciative.

Get to cook for him--, *him*? Maybe his blood sugar was dropping or something, but where is the attitude of appreciation or gratitude?

Perhaps the ownness is on us givers because some acts of kindness are actually sacrifices for us. If we let the person know that then where is the heart of giving? It then becomes more of a *quid pro quo*, or you will **owe** me later act. Still, if you sacrifice to bless another person who is unsaved, they will behave as unsaved people behave. Entitled. Impatient. Rude. Well that establishes them as a taker. If you are doing this kindness as unto the Lord, or you've been sent by the Lord to bless this soul, then so be it. Do what God says and keep it moving.

Making nachos was a sacrifice because I could have been doing something else more enjoyable, such as studying the Word instead of being in the kitchen.

This was a grown person, not a child, but you don't think he said, *Thank you, do you?*

What did I do? I made the nachos at my regular speed with a good attitude and smiled. If, as a Christian I planted the seed of this is how Christians behave, or if I *watered* a seed that had already been planted by someone else, then so be it. None of us can allow a would-be kind gesture to deteriorate into a shouting match or an opportunity for the devil to get involved.

Whether a soul says, *thank you*, or not we do what the Lord says. And we pay attention to our own manners, as it pertains to gratitude and respect of others, and especially to God.

The Arc of Thank You

Folks look at rainbows and may think of the alleged pot of gold at the end of that colorful arch. But the overarching lesson of thankfulness is that at one end, you have **already** received something, either from the Lord or from someone that God has inspired to bless you, be kind to you, or show you favor. Was what you received of value to you? Did it bless you? Have you already received a pot of gold, unexpectedly?

But at the other end of that arc is ***Thanksgiving***, where you are thankful, you show gratitude and appreciation. The back end of that arc usually starts with a *thank you.* Perhaps that *thank you* is the real pot of gold.

In polite society, that *thank you* used to be a thank you note. Today, we could at least send a thank you text, but **saying** *thank you* is the most powerful form of all.

The words that God speaks, they are Spirit, and they are life. We are to behave as Jesus did, so our spoken words are powerful. A spoken thank you comes from the heart and out of the heart flows the issues of life.

This book is not about pots of gold, it is about the Gates of

Thanksgiving. There is a gate, and at the gate there is an entrance. The cost, the only cost of entering through that gate is thanksgiving, a grateful heart, an appreciative attitude will get you through that gate.

Strongmen or Strongholds at the Gate

There are many gates in the spirit.

If we do a word study of *gates* in the Bible, we will see that *gate* or *gates* are mentioned at least 350 times. There are gates to cities which afforded protection for the people who lived within that city. They needed protection against marauding tribes and armies.

Even today people put walls and gates around their homes and compounds for both privacy and protection.

Gates most often protect something, either people or things. A gate was put up so Adam and Eve did not return to the Garden at Eden but were forced to abide by their eviction.

The devil has put up gates as well. So many gates in the Spirit are blocked against us. There are good things in that gate or beyond that gate for us, but they are blocked. Else the Psalmists would never have said in Psalm 24, *Lift up ye heads, oh ye gates and the King of Glory shall come in.*

Some of those gates have been erected by the enemy and there are strongmen guarding those gates and blocking God's people from entering. You may know that I write a lot on spiritual warfare, however, this book is about Thanksgiving.

There are no strongmen **at** the Gates of the Lord. We can enter in through those Gates *with* Thanksgiving.

The problem is not anything that is external to us, there are no guards standing at the Gates of Thanksgiving to keep us from coming in. The problem is what may be ***in*** us. Idols in our souls may have taken positions to block our hearing, seeing, understanding, and or ability to forgive, putting up strongholds to keep us out of places that God has for us. That essentially keeps us away from blessings and blessings away from us.

For example, we can look at others and as I declared at the start of this book, there are those who don't say, *Thank you*, when you surely would think they should. You hold a door for them, you let them go ahead of you in traffic, or you stop and let someone cross the street. A verbal *thank you* might not always be expedient, but a wave is commonly understood as a *thank you*.

As said, there are no strongmen blocking us from entering into Thanksgiving and therefore coming through the Gates of the Lord. The problem would be what *spirits* are **_in_** us that make us dull, numb, ungrateful, unappreciative, or arrogant? What *spirits* might be in us that would make us think that God should be doing this that or the other for us, or the nerve to be angry thinking that God didn't do this that or the other for us, or that He didn't do it fast enough.

Since this book is written during holiday season, I am praying for people who are angry and bitter at God because they lost something or someone that they didn't want to lose. That can be devastating and life changing. Those feelings can be exacerbated during certain seasons of the year. The problem is that if a person gets stuck in the stages of grief --, stuck at blame--, and are blaming God, they are harboring a *spirit* or *spirits* that essentially are anti-Christ.

For your consideration, the Stages of Grief:

- Denial
- Anger: *Why did this happen? Who is to blame?*
- Bargaining

- Depression
- Acceptance

If you are angry at God, or hate God, then you are anti-Christ. All these types of *spirits* will keep you from Thanksgiving and will keep you from entering in through the Gates of Thanksgiving.

This is how the devil wants it because through those Gates is where your questions will be answered, your answers will be found, and your healing will be--, yes, your emotional healing and soul restoration.

So, even if there is no strongman at the door, at the gate, the *spirits* inside of you are behaving as internal strongmen keeping you from exactly what you need which is just beyond those Gates of Thanksgiving.

There is a **stronghold**, and it is *inside* you.

The Gates of the Lord are available to us, and the entrance fee is thanksgiving. As long as the *spirits,* idols, that is, demons in your soul don't keep you back, you can be thankful and **enter *in*.**

A Heart of Thanksgiving

That entrance fee is not just lip service, but a true heart of thanksgiving is required. Remember when your parents made you say, *Sorry* to your brother, but you really didn't mean it? Oh, how many times through your childhood did you do that? Yeah, it's not that. A fake thanksgiving won't get you in.

I recall one Sunday morning at church I was in morning warfare prayer to open up the service. The *spirit of thanksgiving* came over me so strongly that I was thankful for everything--, every little thing and those thanks just poured out of my mouth. I was thankful for daily bread, food to eat, those who grew it, harvested it, and those who packaged and drove the trucks to deliver it to us. The Holy Spirit had me praying for the drivers of those trucks. I couldn't help it.

People thought I was nuts. I wasn't, and I am not.

> When the Spirit of the Lord comes upon my heart, I will dance like David danced. (Fred Hammond)

When the *spirit of thanksgiving* comes upon you, you will be heartily thankful for all that God has done for you, every little thing.

Thanksgiving is not a few *thank you's* until you feel a certain way, or feel better, or feel like enough people or the right people have heard you. It is the heart of thanksgiving that employs and engages your soul that gets you into the Gates of Thanksgiving.

So many folks love to say that if the Lord never does another thing for them, that they'd be satisfied right now. That sounds like an abundance of gratitude talking and we hope that is true. After all, humans are famous for believing they will never be hungry again after eating a large meal. But 4 hours later...

We should never think we will not need anything more from God because we need Him every day, and every hour.

Let Me In

There are gated communities that we can't get into. There are gated office complexes, gated compounds where we can't get in unless we are invited, or we are members.

There are gates in the spiritual world erected by the enemy to keep us away from the blessings that God has for us. If we don't know the password or the passcode, we can't get in. If we don't know the requirements at the gate, the Enemy may block us from getting in. With the Enemy, the requirements vary--, it's like a game of Rumpelstiltskin; it's a puzzle that he doesn't want you to solve, or some evil that you are asked to do, required to do, don't want to do, and never should do.

But the key to getting into the gates of the Lord is *Thanksgiving*. plain and simple, *Thanksgiving*. If that was ever a secret withheld from you before, it is no more.

People are not thankful as they used to be – they don't even say *thank you* like they used to – it could be because people don't talk as much as in times past. Everyone is on a cellphone. People are wearing masks and social distancing. Still, gratitude is in fashion with God, and it should be with one another in the Faith, as well.

You might give someone your lunch while remaining hungry yourself, they will tell you what was wrong with the sandwich and never say, *thank you.* You could give someone your last dollar, and they may turn and ask, *Is that all you have?* You may give someone your seat on the train and never be acknowledged, as if they deserve a seat, and you don't.

Give not that which is holy unto the dogs, neither cast ye your pearls before swine, lest they trample them under their feet, and turn again and rend you, (Matthew 7:6).

An ungrateful *spirit*, a *spirit* of ingratitude is very unbecoming to the LORD; it is off putting, and sometimes offensive. God has done so much for us, can we not just say, *Thank You?* Please remember that you may be called to ungrateful souls in your ministry and in your Christian walk. Ours is not to judge them; we obey God. I reiterate this book is about you, the reader, the child of God. It is not a book to pass judgment on the ill-mannered of the world, because God loves them, and He so loved you.

This book is about all who are invited and given opportunities and impetus to enter into Thanksgiving every day--, the wise child of God will accept that invitation.

We Are Invited

The Gates of the LORD is not an evil gate set against us; we may simply enter into His gates with Thanksgiving. These gates automatically keep the murmurers and the complainers out because their heart, their attitude is not right. This is not to exclude anyone; it is to protect the *spirit* of the place.

Certainly, you have noticed that one complainer can spoil an entire event or day. One sinner can do much harm. At your workplace have you noticed that one dissenter can ruin the entire morale of the team. Actually, that one may be the *cause* of a group of employees never becoming a team, or provoke the dismantling of a team.

Recently, in a certain office, there was a new hire. Two of the other employees who had been there for a while had a violent reaction to the new hire. The new employee was friendly enough, very competent and no nonsense. Well, this disrupted the lazy, nonsensical, but hidden work patterns the other two had.

A war of emotions quickly ignited. No, the workplace did not implode, the previous two employees lost their jobs. Not before they launched an all-out two-pronged campaign to cast aspersion on the new hire and get rid of the new worker; but it all backfired and the veteran two ended up out the door.

The manager of that business would not let the unwarranted anger, hostility, and ire ruin the atmosphere of the workplace. Someone, or someone's had to go.

The atmosphere of the realms of God, is protected because those who behave in an evil way obviously have evil *spirits* with them, and those *spirits* cannot enter in. God is way more efficient at discerning evil *spirits* than we are, and often we, as Christians give people the benefit of the doubt, if there is any doubt.

When a person is seeking a job, they will always be on their best behavior; they send their *representative* to the interview. Then, when they feel threatened about the job that they have and are not doing --, the real person shows up. At that time managers and HR wonder how that person ever got hired, or they think this person has really *changed.*

God doesn't even let evil into His realm because once in, that *spirit* will attempt to ruin the atmosphere, and God is not having that. Didn't the devil already get kicked out of Heaven for that?

And he said unto them, I beheld Satan as lightning fall from heaven, (Luke 10:18).

For this same reason, saints of God, we can know that certain *spirits* will never get in through the Gates of Thanksgiving, the Gates of Heaven, into the Kingdom of God. Those *spirits* are evidenced by the ungodly behavior of those who carry them.

Ungodly *spirits* attempt to impart their nature into humans, this is how they show themselves, and this is how we can recognize their presence.

Pretty is as pretty does--, not as pretty looks, because pretty on the surface will only look—pretty. In that office situation we just discussed, *Pretty* came to the interview, but **Pretty Ugly** raised its head when it felt threatened about losing their job.

God looks deeper than flesh, and so must we, because beauty is only skin deep.

Past these gates there is a realm that we are invited into, that we may enter freely. Once inside these gates, in this realm we may partake of whatever is in that realm.

So, we are now ***in***. Amen.

In the Spirit just as in the natural, gates are there to keep folks out, or protect the folks, the people and the things that are in there. There are some things that are only for chosen people. What is inside the Gates of Thanksgiving is only for God's people. It is the entrance to the Courts of the Lord.

Ungrateful Heart

Instead of the two previous employees being thankful for their jobs at a very pleasant place to work, with a nice salary, they instead tried to stage an insurgency, group together and rebel against the new employee, mainly because they thought that one of the two of them would lose their job because of her. Seems they wanted *status quo* and to work together more than they cared about the business they worked for, or to do the job and create a career for themselves.

Neither of them was slated to lose their jobs, but they thought so--, probably because they didn't perform their work duties very well, and sometimes not at all--, hiding undone work in the strangest places. Perhaps they felt guilty, and saw the handwriting on the wall, that wasn't even there. Yet. The scenario they created was a self-fulfilling evil prophecy and they each individually and in tandem caused the other to lose their job.

Within a week of the new employee's arrival, they accused the new hire of stealing money from the purse of one of the older employees. That is a serious accusation that pushes all things to the limit, because it means that one--, either the accuser or the one accused will lose their job. Depending on the amount stolen and if this can be proved, worse things could happen if the criminal justice system was called into this situation, but alas, it was $10. that was alleged to be stolen.

That seems like a small amount, but when money is your *god*, when money is your idol, which was evident in Employee B--, there was a violent accusation and response to the alleged theft of this money. There was no calming Employee B down, they went on a rampage. This forced the manager's hand--, Employee B had to be let go, as they could not prove the robbery, and Employee B was disrupting the entire business.

Worse, Employee B was egged on by Employee A who pretty much knew that B would be fired for such an outburst and then Employee A would have played witch-chess again and kept her job. The only thing A didn't realize is that management was on to Employee A's game--, A had "gotten rid" of three other new hires over the last few months.

Employee A and Employee B were ungrateful and evil--, jealous, disrespectful, unthankful. You can't even enter into a job with that attitude --, those attitudes. That is a good way of putting it – evil *spirits* **cause** evil attitudes --, that's how we recognize that at least something is not right, but it is also how we recognize that they are present in people. Evil *spirits* want their host (victim) to take on their nature. Many times, they are successful.

But there is deliverance.

So, if you can't even get into a job with those *spirits*, there is no way you can enter in through the Gates of the Lord, the Gates of Thanksgiving with those demons on board.

It's A Realm

Holy Spirit spoke to me today, saying, **Thanksgiving is a realm.** Through the Gates of Thanksgiving is the Realm of Thanksgiving. Thanksgiving is a **PLACE**.

This book is written as an outcropping of the American holiday, Thanksgiving, which I've nicknamed, National Carbohydrate Day. There is nothing wrong with

Thanksgiving, but it is more than a once-a-year thing. Most people that I've met from other countries and cultures adore this day and will quickly say that it's their favorite holiday, I feel that is because they are not offended by anything particularly religious or spiritual about it. Please--, it's become a celebration of food, football, and the prospects of shopping. What's not to like? You get a day off, and for many—two days off, and then the weekend, feeding your flesh all the while.

  The Gates of Thanksgiving is a whole other thing. You are escorted into the Realm of Thanksgiving <u>with</u> and <u>*by*</u> Thanksgiving. As said before, this realm requires a key or passcode--, that being the giving of thanks, a grateful heart, a *spirit of gratitude*. **<u>This takes humility.</u>**

Proud people do not say, *Thank you*, not to people and if they don't say it to people do we think that they are saying it to God? If you can't say, *thank you* to your brother whom you have seen, are we to believe you are saying, *Thank You* to God whom you have not seen?

Still, it takes thankfulness and gratitude to God to enter into the Realm of Thanksgiving.

What is a realm? A realm is a kingdom. It is a domain, a sphere. In spiritual terms, a realm is beyond the physical; it is invisible, unless you can see in the spirit. Some can see in the spirit; they are seers. No, you are not weird, if you are a seer.

Some can hear in the spirit – they may not see anything, but they can hear --. No, you are not crazy, you are one who hears spiritual things. A warning here is that the Enemy sends in dark *spirits*, and they are very chatty. So you have to try everything you "hear" with the Word of God and with prayer so you know "who" said it to you.

Some can both see and hear in spiritual realms.

Some can even smell in the spirit.

Some can do all of that, and even more as their gifting and the Spirit of God allows. Whatever gifting you have, it must be properly honed and used, else the Enemy will try to hijack it, steal it to use for evil.

We are to stir up our gifts and we do that in our salvation by receiving and submitting to the Holy Spirit, reading the Word of God, entering into Praise & Worship, and praying in the Spirit. Obeying the Word and abiding by the disciplines of the faith such as tithing, giving, and participating in dedicated fasts is part of proper Christian training, especially for release into service and ministry to others. Be sure to dedicate your fasts, else they are only diets, or they can be turned into evil fasts.

Is not this the kind of fasting I have chosen: to loose the chains of injustice and untie the cords of the yoke, to set the oppressed free and break. (Isaiah 58:6).

10,000 Tongues

The psalmist says that if he had 10,000 tongues, that is, if he could speak 10,000 different languages, it wouldn't be enough to say, *Thank You* to the LORD for all that He has done for him.

Danke, thank you, gracias, merci, obrigada—knowing all those languages but would it ever be enough to really thank God?

How much, how many *thank you's* is enough to gain admission to this Realm?

Well, not to cross the psalmists, but it is the words spoken out of our mouth, but it is **more** than just the words, it is the heart of Thanksgiving that gets us into the Realm of Thanksgiving. It is the *heart* of the grateful that stirs the heart of God. In Scriptures we are told that God looks at the heart, while man tends to look at the outward appearance of others.

At our Thanksgiving feasts, it is not the green bean and sweet potato casserole or the massive turkey. Just as mom and dad, grandma and grandpa are surely far more excited to see the family coming to visit, coming together, rather than the traditional menu that they have probably had every year for the past 60, 70, or more years – since *they* were children.

For young folks it's hard to believe that food gets old, but eating the same thing over and again does lose its shine after a while. Grown people are interested in relationships and seeing their loved ones more than they care about the food.

Your folks and grand-*folks* are glad to see you, the grandchildren, the children are glad to see the parents and grandparents and the cousins – that's the heart of the day. I'm not accusing anyone of other sentiments. This book is about entering in to the Realm of Thanksgiving with that true heart that God loves.

No, I haven't said anything about family disputes or escalations at holidays –especially when alcohol is involved, but that can be an unfortunate reality. Even if the true *spirit of thanksgiving* was present at such a gathering – one sinner can destroy much good. Some family gatherings deteriorate and sadly so. But we are in this world and not *of* it, so we have to guard our own hearts and the *spirits* that we allow to affect us.

Go to your family events; and go prayed up, and with the right *spirit*, in the Name of Jesus.

We really want to enter into the Realm of Thanksgiving, so we must persist.

Therefore, your mature relatives look on the heart of those who come to Thanksgiving in the natural, as does God look at the heart—not just that you came, your appearance, what you wore, your shoes or your hairdo. God looks at the heart and discerns, Is this true Thanksgiving?

If it is, if God judges that it is, **<u>then enter in.</u>**

Wholeness

What is in this Realm of Thanksgiving? One thing is: Wholeness.

In the Thanksgiving Realm is **Wholeness**. We know this because there were 10 lepers who were all healed and one came back to say, *Thank you*. The other nine former lepers walked away, going about their business to do whatever they wanted to do. Of course, they had to go show themselves to the priest to be allowed back in society, but after that, surely, they were going to do *whatever*. Perhaps they had been away from their families too long and missed them terribly. Perhaps they had work to do or businesses to run.

But one former leper turned back, and came back to say, *Thank you* to Jesus. And in so doing that former disease-ridden man **agreed** with this realm of Heaven, the Realm of Thanksgiving. We don't know how long he lingered. We don't know how long it takes to say, *Thank you*. We don't know how long it took that particular man to say, *Thank You.*

Thank you's can be brief or extended. *Thank you's* can be just a walk by and a wave or the presentation of a gift, or the offering of a service. *You've done this for me, what can I do for you?*

We don't know how long this man stayed in the Realm of Thanksgiving – but even if it was just a second, or just for a few seconds, he agreed with Heaven and **entered *in*.**

Healing came to him and to the other nine as well. But as he tarried in Thanksgiving this one man got more, so much more – he became whole.

Were the other nine never whole in the first place? Were the other nine ignorant that they could become whole? Were the other nine simply ungrateful? Were they arrogant, or prideful? Were they filled with other *spirits* that drove them away from the presence of He who could make them whole? The Bible doesn't say, but this is all for your consideration.

One man came back, entered into the Realm of Thanksgiving simply by saying, *Thank You* to the Lord; and that one was made whole.

Wholeness is in this realm through these Gates of Thanksgiving.

Why wholeness?

Because you need **Wholeness** to praise the Lord. With your whole being, you love the Lord. With your *whole* heart, you praise the Lord. With your *whole* soul, you praise the Lord. Praise is what you do in the next Court of the Lord as you escalate into worship.

1. What are the things that are broken, fragmented or need wholeness in your life?

Tell the Lord about it, enter into Thanksgiving and receive what is promised to you in that realm.

2. Where do you need healing?

Where in your body, soul, spirit and within that, where and what in your body has a need? Enter into His Gates with Thanksgiving.

What of your soul needs healing? Enter into His Gates with Thanksgiving.

Is your human spirit broken from all that you've been through in life? Enter into His Gates with Thanksgiving. Wholeness is through that Gate and in that Realm.

Leprosy was the worst, or about the worst named disease of the Bible. It was considered incurable. It was incurable except by miracle touch and deliverance by the Word of God through His Old Testament prophets, and by Jesus Christ and the Disciples. Jesus still heals. The Holy

Spirit is the Spirit of Deliverance, Amen.

Do the things in your life, the things you've been through seem unfixable? Incurable? Enter into His Gates with Thanksgiving.

When you don't feel like being thankful, or don't feel that you have anything to be thankful for; you must be thankful anyway.

Lepers were to sit outside the Gate that is backward and counter-intuitive since *outside* the gate is the place of punishment. In Bible times they considered disease as a result of sin, so humans were punishing other humans for being ill.

Inside the gate is where healing might take place—in the natural, there are doctors inside the gate; Doctors without Borders didn't exist yet. _Inside_ the gates were the priests –and the religious people--, couldn't they pray for these lepers? Of course, outside the gate limited the exposure of the townspeople to the dread disease.

But, these were unsaved people, so they would be thinking the opposite of the way they should be thinking. The Holy Spirit is the Spirit of Wisdom; those people didn't have that yet. But we should have it.

Spiritually, *inside* the Gates, in the realms of the Lord where there is healing and help and hope---, but a person has to **enter *in*.**

Wholeness is in the Realm of Thanksgiving. Yet, with a pure heart, that's not why you're entering in – to get more. I say more because if you are thankful, **you already got**

something, or some things; you are simply, like the healed leper turning back to say, *Thank You--n*ot of a selfish motive to see what else you can get.

Thank you is one of the first things instilled in us by our parents. Diligent parents make toddlers say, *thank you* before they give them cookies and toys, and things.

Not being or feeling appreciated is why when people don't put value on you or what you do for them, you usually stop doing for them. It is human nature to back off if that's the case. It is not unless the Lord provokes you to maintain and continue being good to them will you or most people continue.

In the same way when people are good to you, it is God who

prompts people to show you kindness and favor. Or do you, or I dare think that we are good enough for people to just do good to us all the time?

Do you think God is like that?

No. God shows us Mercy and Grace and favor many times when we don't even deserve it.

For that and so much more, we should be and remain thankful.

The Prophetic Thank You

Sometimes, our *thank You's* to God are prophetic thank you's. Without faith it is impossible to please God. We want God pleased as much or more than we want to be pleased ourselves. Sometimes when there is no corn in the field, or in the barn, we say, *Thank You* to God because we count Him faithful who promised.

Sarah laughed at the promise of righteous seed, Isaac, even though he didn't come until she was about 99 years old. She was not mocking the promise or God; she said, *Shall I have joy again?*

We say, *thank You* because He's done it before, and we know that God will come through. Sometimes it is prophetic because we see it in the distance. Elijah saw a cloud in the distance about the size of a man's hand– and surely for that drought-filled land and for the sake of the Prophet's words, that prophet himself said, *Thank You, Lord.*

Blessed is he who has not seen, yet still believes. That man says, *Thank You* prophetically to the Father. That is faith and it is very pleasing to God.

Faith is not paying on Tuesday for a hamburger today (Wimpy). That is the world's system. Credit and credit cards, where we get it first, then we pay, assuming that payment is a thank you is not faith; it is the opposite of faith.

With God we receive spiritually first, which sometimes looks like nothing to the onlooker, but we say, *Thank You* when we first receive spiritually, then it manifests in the natural. Don't worry, if you didn't see it spiritually first – this time--, God will keep building your faith and opening your spiritual eyes. Especially if you ask and ask in faith, believing God, then no good thing will ever be withheld from you.

I'm from a large family. My sibs often didn't understand how I got my dad to say yes to things I asked for whereas they weren't nearly so successful. Let me tell you how. I'd ask Dad for things at least 2 to three days, or more, in advance of needing it. Then I'd say to him, *I don't need to know right away, but could you think about it and let me know in a couple of days?* Invariably, I would also say, *Thank you, Dad* (for considering my request). Then I'd be done with it.

My Dad, may the Lord rest his soul, would often come through for me. It was perceived that I was his favorite. I don't think I was, but I do not think I wasn't either. It was because I spoke to him with respect, I didn't cajole, or pester him, and I always said, *Thank you* to him when I was asking and when I received.

That was how I approached my natural father from the time that I was 10 or 12 years old. But look what I found in the Word of God a dozen or more years later when I first read the Bible as an adult.

> Be careful for nothing; but in every thing by prayer and supplication with thanksgiving let your requests be made known unto God. And the

peace of God, which passeth all understanding, shall keep your hearts and minds through Christ Jesus, (Philippians 4:6-8).

With thanksgiving.

You want something from God, ask Him. Ask Him in faith, believing it shall be, that it will come to you. Ask Him respectfully and in a well-mannered way. Ask Him with Thanksgiving.

That shows God your faith. Thanksgiving is like saying, I believe I receive. And, Amen.

Pride Stops It

I, me, myself and I--, it is unseemly to brag; that's pride--, the *spirit of pride*. It is tacky to boast. It is ungodly to brag on yourself. Pride is the mouth making up for known, seen, or hidden deficiencies. Wholeness is in our ability to be humble. Because pride doesn't belong in man, when it is not present a person's soul is more likely to be whole, and a whole soul can exemplify meekness and humility.

Let's say you begin helping a person, they don't appreciate it, so *you* stop helping them, or they stop the process by their attitude or obstinance. Let me say *pride* stops the process because *pride* doesn't want a man whole because then *pride* would have no place in that man, in that man's life. Once a man is whole, he kicks *pride* out --, or we can say that pride must be dealt with and put out or cast out for a man's soul to be whole. There is no place for any work of the flesh in a whole soul.

You cannot enter into ***Thanksgiving*** and stay there within your self. Exhibiting **Thanksgiving is** admitting **that there is OTHER than yourself in the world.** *OTHER* is not only <u>**there**</u>, *OTHER* did something for you – something that you discern, something you can understand, see, feel, and appreciate, and remember. Thankful people live happier, more content lives and have better memories, as well.

    Thanksgiving is the first step in realizing that God **_IS_**—God exists. And, because you realize this, the Gates of Thanksgiving are opened, and you have invitation, permission, and authority to enter this realm.

    Really, how can you go to a place that you don't think exists? How or why would you go to the house of a person that you do not believe exists?

    By entering into Thanksgiving, you prove that you realize that God exists.

Welcome

To stay in the Realm of Thanksgiving, you must remain thankful, grateful, acknowledging God, if you fall from thanksgiving and become ungrateful, complaining and murmuring, then the gates may close to you and remain closed until you can again become thankful and then re-ENTER into His Gates with Thanksgiving.

They Became DEAD

We get our food, our daily bread from the Realm of Thanksgiving, and we should eat it there also.

When the Israelites stopped being thankful and started murmuring and complaining in the Wilderness, their *wholeness* was threatened, and they became DEAD. Surely, they had to be thankful to have walked out of Egypt on dry land.

And the children of Israel said unto them, Would to God we had died by the hand of the LORD in the land of Egypt, when we sat by the flesh pots, and when we did eat bread to the full; for ye have brought us forth into this wilderness, to kill this whole assembly with hunger, (Exodus 16:3).

    It defies logic. Why couldn't those people remain thankful that they were freed from slavery? Shouldn't they still have been in a honeymoon period of being in love with God who saved them out of Egypt?

    Well, they should have made God their God. But no--, their bellies were their *gods*, and their bellies were complaining so they opened their own mouths and spoke what their bellies told them to say. Sadly, they ultimately got what they said; they died in the Wilderness.

Had Aaron and Moses not fallen on their faces and prayed to God, interceding, even the children of these complainers would not have been saved.

God's Mercy can be provoked by prayer and proper prayers.

He Gave Thanks

> Then He ordered the crowds to recline on the grass; and He took the five loaves and the two fish, and, looking up to heaven, He gave thanks *and* blessed and broke the loaves and handed the pieces to the disciples, and the disciples gave them to the people,
>
> (Matthew 14:19, AMP)

After Jesus gave thanks, the miracle happened. A miracle for all to see and taste, proving that it was real and tangible. The fish and the loaves fed 2,000 people, 5,000 people--, multitudes. When Jesus prayed, the fish and loaves became WHOLE, and that is even *more* than enough.

We give thanks for our food, so it becomes *more* than enough, and when we use it, *when we eat that food* it doesn't harm or defile us, it makes **us** WHOLE. This is another reason we must pray.

Jesus gave thanks; He entered into a Realm.

Jesus took the entire Multitude to dine in the Realm of Thanksgiving. They dined on fishes and loaves. Jesus Prayed and **HE GAVE THANKS**. The Holy Spirit was not yet released in the Earth. So, what Jesus did was all Jesus--, all God and all Jesus.

Have you ever wondered how that miracle happened?

Jesus Gave Thanks.

That is how it happened; **Jesus Gave Thanks. That was the first Thanksgiving; <u>Jesus Gave Thanks</u>, and then He gave food to the Multitude.**

God so loved the world that He *gave*. Jesus does what He sees the Father do, so Jesus GAVE. Jesus Gave. He gave many things, thanks was just one of those things.

I've always thought that meant that He thanked God, and He did. He gave the <u>Grace</u> of Thanksgiving. Grace is a power. That multitude was empowered to come through these Gates into **Thanksgiving**.

In my book, **Occupy Until I Return** I discussed where Jesus told Peter that Satan wanted to sift him like wheat? Jesus then said, ***But I have prayed for you.***

Jesus prayed to bless the Multitude that day that He also fed them. He was teaching and preaching and healing them. He also, in the natural, He fed them. Everything Jesus did was not in the Spirit, it may have started there, but it manifested in the natural. What Jesus did, and asked for came down from Heaven, it came down from the Spirit into the natural.

Jesus prayed.

Praying is powerful and effects mighty changed in the spirit and in the Earth. We follow Jesus; therefore, we also pray.

When Jesus prays, He prays in agreement with Heaven and He brings Heaven down to Earth. Can we do that also? Yes, we should be able to.

We get our food from the Realm of Thanksgiving, and we should eat our meals, take our meals in the Realm of Thanksgiving.

He Showed Us How

After this manner therefore pray ye:
Our Father which art in heaven,
Hallowed be thy name.

Thy kingdom come, Thy will be done
in earth, as it is in heaven. Give us
this day our daily bread.

And forgive us our debts, as we
forgive our debtors.

And lead us not into temptation, but
deliver us from evil: For thine is the
kingdom, and the power, and the
glory, for ever. Amen. (Mtt 6:9-13).

Jesus showed us these steps:

- Acknowledge God with honor.
- Ask for the Kingdom of God. A realm is a kingdom. Ask that Earth agrees with Heaven.
- Jesus taught them to ask for daily bread. Bread is food, manna, and sustenance, but deliverance is also *the children's bread*. Jesus is the Bread of Heaven. Ask what you will and if you abide in the Lord, it shall be given to you.
- Ask for forgiveness; to be forgiven, we repent.
- We are to forgive others – forgiveness and repentance causes evil *spirits* to drop off of you and out of your life.

With this formula, you can **enter in.**

The Grace of Thanksgiving

Jesus gave the Grace of Thanksgiving, so the multitude was *empowered* to come through the Gates, into Thanksgiving. Whether the Multitude knew it or not, it happened. All they may have known, being carnal, is that they ate.

If only the Israelites coming out of Egypt had realized that the prayers and actions of Moses, who was used as a prophet of God entered those former slaves into a **realm** where the Red Sea was parted, and they all walked through on dry land. The power of prayer. Prayer brings realms to Earth. Let it be done on Earth as it is in Heaven.

Jesus by His prayer bestowed the Realm of Thanksgiving upon the Multitude, so they **dined** in the Realm of Thanksgiving that day. Did they go there, in the spirit, or did the Realm come down at Jesus' request?

The Book of Revelation says, *I saw the New Jerusalem coming down from above.*

Jesus came from Heaven to Earth to show the way. Things come from the Spirit into the natural. Things come from Heaven to Earth. We do not dictate to God what should be happening in Heaven; what happens in Earth does not happen in Heaven.

The Third Heaven holds all precedent to anything we could think or ask to happen on this planet.

The Bible also says, *Let it be done on Earth as it is in Heaven.*

We serve a God of order; Jesus told the Disciples to organize and seat this multitude of people by rows. With God, all things should be done decently and in order. Jesus said the grace—. Grace is a power. By that power, He bestowed *Thanksgiving* on the Multitude that were seated there that day.

The Multitude was seated; they didn't go anywhere. **Jesus brought Heaven down to them that day and they dined in a realm that was not**

before known or historically recorded on Earth.

That was a powerful miracle. By His hand, we all are fed. Jesus, the Bread of Heaven. Jesus, the Right Hand of God. By His Hand, we all are fed.

Jesus also proved by this miracle, ***Where I am you may be also.***

The Power of Thanksgiving

With words, Jesus multiplied fish and loaves, exceedingly. He gave thanks; see the power in thankfulness.

Now that you've entered in through the Gates of Thanksgiving, never doubt ever again that you can *enter in* wherever you need to enter in. That is in any kind of Gate for any reason, by the power and the authority of Jesus Christ – His Name, and His Blood. You are more than a conqueror.

By His Grace

As we pray like Jesus, and as Jesus instructed and demonstrated, we say grace, we pray grace, therefore all who sit at our table are invited into the Gates of Thanksgiving, by *our* Thanksgiving, by our authority, by our invitation, …which is authorized for us by Jesus Christ.

So, like a gated community when the gate opens, those who are with the person with the passcode can also ***enter in.***

We say grace, we ask the Grace, as your parents may have taught you, not just every day, but every meal. Thanksgiving is not a once-a-year thing. We bless the table, the hands that cooked it, we bless the people gathered around, we are bestowing ***Grace*** upon them – grace to partake of more than enough daily bread, manna, food, sustenance.

In Philippians. 1:7 Paul states that the Philippians are partakers of his GRACE.

The people you pray for, those who sit under your tutelage, your prayers, intercession, are partakers of your Grace. We are all partakers of the Lord's Grace, but the people whom we sit under, those who have authority over us, our leaders and pastors, and teachers--, we partake of their Grace, as well.

We aren't feeding 2,000 or 5,000 necessarily, maybe four, or five, or six --, and a few times a year on special occasions, or holidays, up to 10, or 15 or 20. If we remember to pray and extend the Grace that is imparted to us, those who sit at our table can receive of what we receive from the Lord.

To whom are you extending GRACE? Who is partaking of your power by your invitation? To whom are you inviting into the Realm of Thanksgiving, where you should be always, or have full access to?

Whom have you invited into the Realm of Salvation with Christ Jesus?

All Day

Spend the day with the Lord. Can you be thankful for a whole day? Can you remember God all day – for a whole day? Giving thanks puts you in place to think about God, to remember Him all day. He's thinking about you, shouldn't you also be thinking of Him?

Thou wilt keep him in perfect peace, whose mind is stayed on thee: because he trusteth in thee,
(Isaiah 26:3)

At the Communion Table

Lord Jesus: I believe in You and thank You for dying for us to be saved. At this communion table, I ask you to show me where I have not been thankful or grateful, and let me repent; Lord hear my prayers, in the Name of Jesus. Let me be grateful for all You have done and even for the kindness of people toward me.

May your Mercy, your Love and Grace wash over me, and speak

for me in every aspect of my life, through Your precious Blood.

I take communion today and I remember Your death, -- until You Come again. I remember your **invitation** to me into the Gates of Thanksgiving, into Salvation, into *sonship*.

This bread now is Your flesh, this wine now is Your precious Blood. I confess that the very life of God, the eternal life and abundant life will flow into me and flow through me.

For I pass on to you what I received from the Lord himself. On the night when he was betrayed, the Lord Jesus took bread and gave thanks to God for it. Then He broke it and said, This is my body which is given for you. Do this in remembrance of me, (1 Corinthians 11:23-26).

Jesus took the cup and the bread, and after He had blessed it, He invited those at the table into His *Realm*.

They all accepted except one, Judas.

Except Judas

The one who did not enter in to that Realm of the Last Supper, Judas, did not receive wholeness. Instead, he ended up DEAD like the complainers in the Wilderness.

We pray that those who are invited, all those we invite to the supper will accept.

Let us consider that Judas could not **enter *in*.** Selling Jesus out, Judas had the *spirit of anti-Christ* on the throne of his heart. How could he enter into the realm where Jesus was? Any of us should be surprised that he could even sit at that table. If it had not have been for God's plan for salvation of mankind, I don't believe Judas could have dined with Jesus and those Disciples on the night that He was betrayed.

He Took the Bread

Jesus took the bread and gave thanks to God for it; He broke it and gave thanks, and that is why there is enough Jesus for all of us. There is more than enough because **HE GAVE THANKS,** and invited us (mankind) into His realm, where we can abide.

As He fed the Multitudes--, and there are still multitudes, billions who need to call on the Name of the Lord, and partake of His Grace, His suffering, His crucifixion, resurrection, and ascension. There is more than enough Jesus for us all because in the Realm of Thanksgiving, there is Wholeness, where we are made whole, we are made new, we are healed by His stripes, and He is also made Whole over and again because those who Give Thanks are allowed into the Realm that makes the miracle of **wholeness** for mankind.

… the Lord Jesus took bread and gave thanks to God for it. Then He broke it and said, This is my body which is given for you. Do this in remembrance of me Jesus took the bread and gave thanks to God for it, and He broke it and gave thanks,

(1 Corinthians 11:24-26).

TAKE THE BREAD

In the same way he took the cup of wine after supper saying, This cup is the new Covenant between God and His people. It is an agreement confirmed with My Blood, do this in remembrance of me as often as ye drink it. For every time you eat this bread and drink this cup, you are announcing the Lord's death until he comes again.

DRINK THE WINE

O give thanks to the Lord of lords: For his mercy endureth for ever. To him who alone doeth great wonders: For his mercy endureth for ever. To him that by wisdom made the heavens: For his mercy endureth for ever. To him that stretched out the earth above the waters: For his mercy endureth for ever. Psalm 136

And we give thanks and enter into the Realm of Thanksgiving where there is help, healing, and **wholeness** by the precious Blood of Jesus.

Amen.

Dear Reader

May the Lord richly bless you for acquiring and reading this book. May you ever enter into the Gates of Thanksgiving, and receive of the Lord, of His Grace, His Mercy, His provision, health, and wholeness, in the Name of Jesus.

Amen.

Dr. Marlene Miles

Other books by this author

AK: The Adventures of the Agape Kid

AMONG SOME THIEVES

Ancestral Powers

Blindsided: *Has the Old Man Bewitched You?*

https://a.co/d/5O2fLLR

Churchzilla, The Wanna-Be, Supposed-to-be Bride of Christ

Demons Hate Questions

Devil Weapons: Unforgiveness, Bitterness,

Dream Defilement

Don't Refuse Me, Lord (4 book series)

Every Evil Bird

Evil Touch

Fantasy Spirit Spouse

FAT Demons (The): *Breaking Demonic Curses*

The Fold (4 book series)

    The Fold (Book 1)

    Name Your Seed (Book 2)

    The Poor Attitudes of Money (3)

    Do Not Orphan Your Seed (4)

    For the Sake of the Gospel (5)

got HEALING? Verses for Life
https://a.co/d/c2zPPOD

got LOVE? Verses for Life
https://a.co/d/iK8LqH3

got HOPE? Verses for Life

got money?

How to Dental Assist

How to Dental Assit2: Be Productive, Not Wasteful

Let Me Have A Dollar's Worth

Living for the NOW of God

Lose My Location
https://a.co/d/crD6mV9

Man Safari, *The*

Marriage Ed. Rules of Engagement & Marriage

Made Perfect in Love

Motherboard (The) - soul prosperity series

Plantation Souls

Power Money: Nine Times the Tithe

The Power of Wealth *(forthcoming)*

Rules of Engagement & Marriage

Seasons of Grief

Seasons of War

Soul Prosperity soul prosperity series 3

https://a.co/d/5p8YvCN

Souls Captivity soul prosperity series 2

The Spirit of Poverty

This Is NOT That: How to Keep Demons from Coming At You

Throne of Grace: Courtroom Prayer

Time Is of the Essence

Too Many Wives: *Why You Have Lady Problems*

Tormenting Spirits
https://a.co/d/dAogEJf

Triangular Power *(series)*

    Powers Above

    SUNBLOCK

    Do Not Swear by the Moon

    STARSTRUCK

Uncontested Doom

Upgrade: How to Get Out of Survival Mode

Toxic Souls (Book 2 of series)

Legacy (Book 3 of series)

Warfare Prayer Against Beauty Curses

Warfare Prayer Against Poverty

What Have You to Declare?

When the Devourer is Rebuked

The Wilderness Romance *(series)*

- *The Social Wilderness*
- *The Sexual Wilderness*
- *The Spiritual Wilderness*